The Old Welsh Way

# Crime and Punishment

Catrin Stevens

Illustrated by Robin Lawrie

# CONTENTS

# Crime and punishment

We, and the society in which we live, need rules to help us to live together in harmony. But, sometimes people commit a crime and break these rules or laws. People have to be punished for breaking the law. The main crimes today – manslaughter, murder, theft and assault – are similar to crimes throughout the ages. But, no-one is persecuted (punished and ill-treated) today for being a witch or for being poor. These days, offenders are punished for driving too fast or for computer fraud.

Punishments have changed a great deal over the centuries. In the old days, the emphasis was on painful corporal (physical) punishment – such as hanging, burning or execution. In 1969, Britain abolished capital punishment (killing someone for offending). In the past, prisoners of war were tortured or made into slaves. But, since 1900 the Geneva Convention has protected the rights of prisoners of war. Today, the main punishments for all kinds of law-breaking are imprisonment and fines (paying a sum of money).

**Discovery of a body – police investigate**

**Four arrested for drug smuggling**

**Speed cameras catch many drivers**

**Man found guilty of shooting a policeman**

**How do we know?**

The history of criminals, their crimes and their punishments can be found in the records of courts of law or in prison registers. Crime stories have also filled newspapers since Victorian times, and these days there are endless such stories on radio and television. Often – especially in the case of women – it's easier to find the history of someone who has broken the law than someone who has always lived a good life.

In order to find out which laws have been broken, we can look at Hywel Dda's laws for the Middle Ages, and from that time onwards we can look at the records of Parliament, in Westminster, London. The Parliament used to pass all the different laws.

A picture of the judge from one of the manuscripts of Hywel Dda's Laws – Peniarth 28

The records for Caernarfonshire Quarter Sessions (a court that met four times a year) in 1563, note that John ab Ieuan of Ceidio had stolen an axe worth four pence. He was whipped and put in the pillory (a wooden frame with holes for the head and hands) as a punishment for the theft.

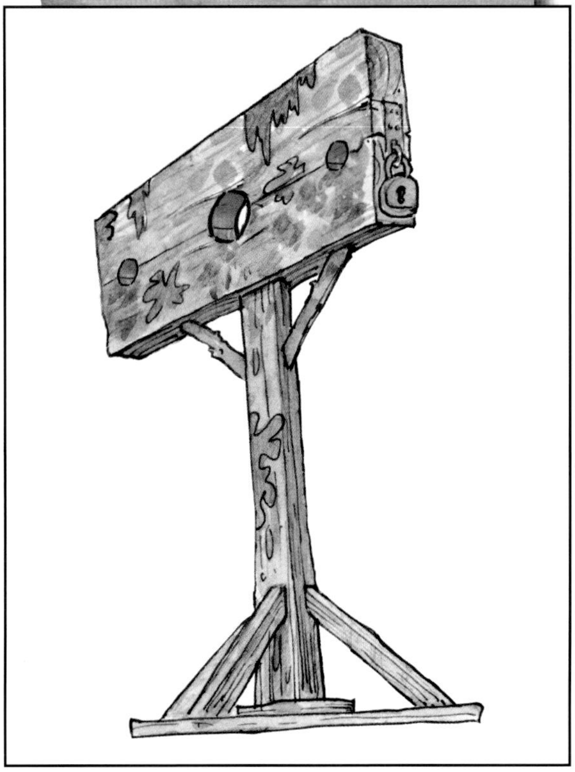

Some strange laws have been passed:

- According to the Laws of Hywel Dda, a wife could divorce (separate legally from) her husband if he had foul (bad) smelling breath!
- In the Age of Elizabeth I, people were fined for not going to church.
- The Puritans passed a law in 1644 forbidding people from celebrating Christmas!

The felons' (criminals') register for Carmarthen prison (1844-1871) tells us a great deal about its prisoners. David Miles from Llandeilo was only thirteen years old when he was imprisoned for stealing shoes in 1869. According to the description he had 'a fresh face' and there is a picture of him in the register. His punishment was to do six days of hard labour (hard work) and to be whipped seventeen times.

Some crimes, such as child abuse and domestic violence, never came to court. These were called domestic (belonging to the home) crimes and policemen didn't like to interfere in people's home lives.

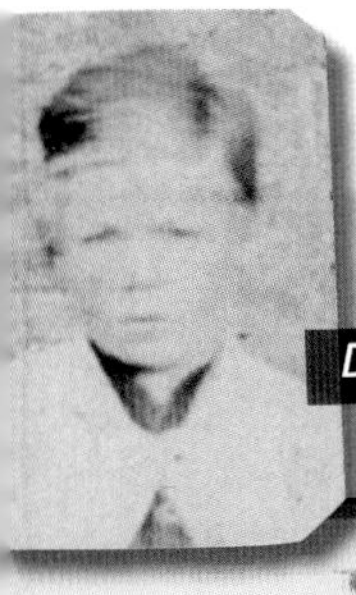

David Miles

A page from Carmarthen prison's register

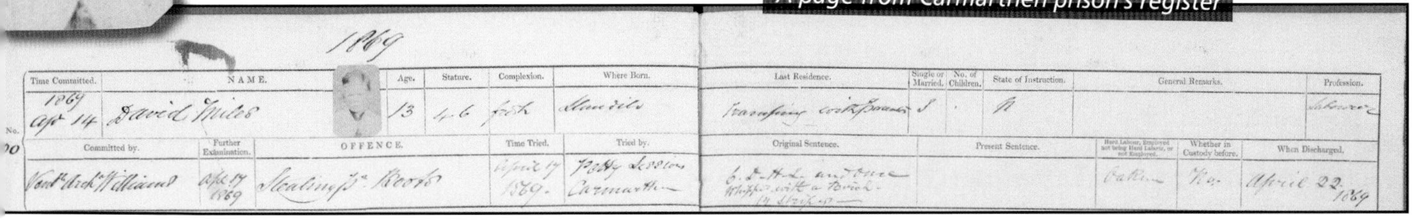

1869

| No. | Time Committed. | NAME. | Age. | Stature. | Complexion. | Where Born. | Last Residence. | Single or Married. | No. of Children. | State of Instruction. | General Remarks. | Profession. |
|---|---|---|---|---|---|---|---|---|---|---|---|---|
| 90 | 1869 Apl 14 | David Miles | 13 | 4 6 | fresh | Llandilo | Travelling with parents | S | . | N | | Labourer |

| Committed by. | Further Examination. | OFFENCE. | Time Tried. | Tried by. | Original Sentence. | Present Sentence. | Hard Labour, Employed not being Hard Labour, or not Employed. | Whether in Custody before. | When Discharged. |
|---|---|---|---|---|---|---|---|---|---|
| Revd Archd Williams | Apl 17 1869 | Stealing 3 Boots | April 17 1869. | Petty Sessions Carmarthen | 6 D. H.L. and once whipped with a Birch 17 strokes | | Oakum | No. | April 22 1869 |

# The Laws of Hywel Dda

During the Middle Ages in Wales, the Laws of Hywel Dda ruled how people should live and behave towards one another. Hywel Dda ruled as king over most of Wales between around 940-950 AD. The law books say that Hywel called together six men from every commote (area) in Wales to Whitland to discuss the country's laws. They decided to keep some of the old laws, to improve some of them and to create some new laws.

Unfortunately, we're not quite sure whether this actually happened. The manuscripts which describe this meeting were written around 1250 AD; that is, at least 300 years after Hywel Dda's death.

It's obvious too that some later laws, which belonged to the thirteenth century, have become mixed up with the early laws in the manuscripts.

But, historians also point out that Hywel Dda is the only king in Welsh history who has been called *Da* ('the Good') and perhaps he was given this name because he taught the Welsh people how to live in harmony.

Today there is a beautiful centre and gardens at Whitland in Carmarthenshire to commemorate and to celebrate the Welsh Laws.

## The Laws of Alfred the Great

A little before the time of Hywel Dda, the famous king, Alfred the Great of Wessex had made laws for the Saxons. Hywel probably knew about these. Yet the Welsh laws are different from those of the Saxons.

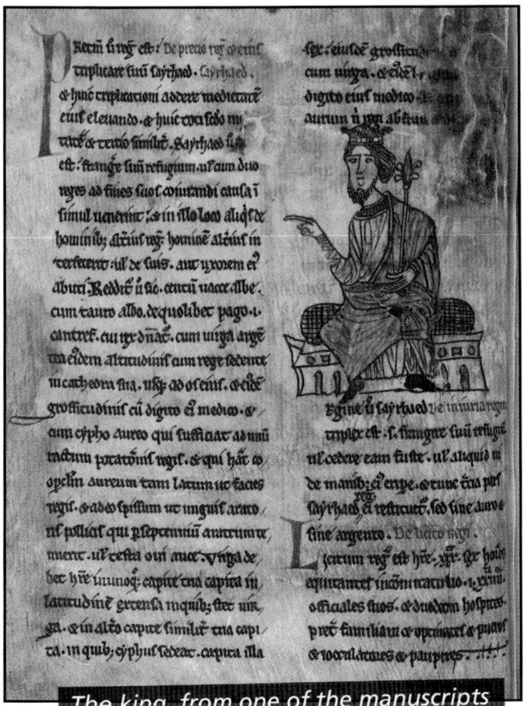

*The king, from one of the manuscripts of Hywel Dda's Laws – Peniarth 28*

*A statue of Hywel Dda in National Museum Wales*

If a thief could prove that he was poor and that he had been begging, unsuccessfully, for three days before stealing food to feed his family, he would not be hanged.

## Paying a murder fee (*galanas*)

According to the Welsh Laws a murderer was not hanged or executed. Instead of this, the murderer's family had to pay a fee to the murdered person's family. This was called *talu galanas*; that is, paying a fine for the value of someone's life. The murder fee for the head of a household was valued at 189 cattle but the murder fee for a villein (someone who worked the land) was only worth 31 cattle.

## The value of parts of the body

If someone was assaulted, the offender had to pay a fee to the value of the part of the body which had been harmed. And each part of the body had a different value. A finger was valued at 20 pence or one cow; but a thumb was twice this value, that is 40 pence or two cows.

A thief could be hanged for stealing. The laws noted the exact value of everything that could be stolen. An oak tree was valued at 120 pence but a hen was only worth one penny.

If a person accused of murder claimed to be innocent, he had to find 50 people to speak on his behalf.

# Keeping law and order through the ages

From the Middle Ages onwards, as the kings of England conquered Wales bit by bit, English laws were passed to rule Wales too. Hywel Dda's Laws were cast aside. After the death of Llywelyn the Last in 1282, six counties were established with a sheriff in charge of each one. A justice (judge, the chief officer of the law) was appointed for North Wales, and another for the counties of Cardiganshire and Carmarthenshire.

Then, between 1536 and 1542, King Henry VIII decided to unite England and Wales under one law and one Parliament. Now, there were a number of law courts and legal officers to keep law and order. Among them were:

- *The Council of the Marches* which met in Ludlow, over the border in England. The Council looked after the defence of the country. It disappeared in 1688.
- *The Great Sessions* where serious criminals, such as murderers and pirates, were tried by a judge and a jury (a group of people who decided whether someone was guilty or not).
- *The Quarter Sessions* which tried less serious crimes before a Magistrate or Justice of the Peace and a jury. This court would meet once every quarter of the year and it would travel around the main county towns.

In 1971, the Great Sessions and the Quarter Sessions were abolished and the Crown Court established in their place. Today, however, 95% of all the country's criminal cases come before the Bench of Magistrates or Justices of the Peace.

Judge Campbell, Presteigne

In the Middle Ages a sheriff had a great deal of work to do. He had to gather evidence about all kinds of criminals – traitors, murderers and thieves; those who bought or sold stolen meat; those who dyed the skins of stolen cattle and horses; those who stole doves, those who sheared sheep at night, or who stole corn from the fields, and many more.

English was the official language in every law court in Wales after the Act of Union in 1536. But, most Welsh people didn't understand English, and the Judges didn't understand Welsh. Therefore translators were needed, but they weren't very good. It was very difficult, therefore, for a person to have a fair trial. Sometimes, a criminal couldn't even understand his sentence (the court's decision). But, fortunately the jury usually understood Welsh and it tended to free prisoners rather than punish them.

In Presteigne, Powys, they have restored the 'Judge's Lodging' in the town so that we, today, can see how a courtroom, a judge's lodging, the servants' rooms and the prisoners' cells appeared, back in the 1870s. It's possible to see graffiti of prisoners' names and their punishments scratched on the building's wall. In one court case, two workers from Rhaeadr fought over a pair of underpants. Eventually they decided who owned the pants by looking carefully at the special marks on them!

A cell door, Judge's Lodging, Presteigne

Judge's Lodging, Presteigne

# Hello, hello, hello! The history of the police

In the old days there were no policemen to ensure that people kept the country's laws. The head of each household and society itself had to catch criminals. Then, towards the end of the Middle Ages, parishes began to choose one person to serve as a constable on their behalf. There wasn't a special uniform or any pay for this work. The constable kept a record of tramps and caught criminals to bring them to court. Sometimes, a 'hue and cry' had to take place to catch a criminal, as in the case of Richard Cheadle.

By around 1800 the population had grown immensely and it was impossible for parish constables to keep order. Therefore, the Home Secretary, Robert Peel, established a Metropolitan Police force in London in 1829, which paid wages to the constables and made them into a professional force. These were called 'Peelers' or 'Bobbies'.

Between 1841 and 1856, several acts of Parliament were passed to establish police forces in every county. From now on a policeman would wear an official uniform and carry special arms. Police stations opened in towns and villages, and in the beginning a policeman had to be on duty the whole time, with no holidays at all.

Today, the police have to deal with all kinds of criminals – from fast drivers to drug pushers and terrorists. They have the latest electronic equipment, fast cars and helicopters.

*Moses Row, a policeman in Merthyr Tudful in the 1860s*

**Dangerous work!**
A policeman's work could be lonely and dangerous. In Dowlais, near Merthyr Tudful, in 1842, Sergeant Dawkins and PC William Fair tried to arrest three local men for assault. But, a crowd of 150 people began throwing stones at them. One offender jumped on top of Dawkins and bit a piece of his nose almost clean away. Eventually, the offenders were caught in spite of the wild crowd.

**Women in the police force**
Women have only been accepted into the police forces in Wales from about 1945 onwards. Even then, their main responsibilities were to work with children and to direct traffic. But, by 2004 a woman called Barbara Wilding had become Chief Constable of the South Wales Police Authority and 640 policewomen worked for her.

**Richard Cheadle**

In 1650 Colonel Richard Bulkeley was murdered by Richard Cheadle on Lafan Sands, Gwynedd. The parish constable called upon everyone to come to help him catch Cheadle, by chasing him and shouting out loudly as if they were hunting. This was called a 'hue and cry'. In each parish it was the local constable's responsibility to carry on the chase. Cheadle was chased and caught at last at Chester, and hanged in Conwy.

When PC James James joined the Glamorgan Police Force in 1860, he was given a wooden truncheon with Queen Victoria's seal on it. He carried it in a pocket inside his trousers. Policemen were also given a pair of handcuffs, a rattle to summon help and an oil lamp. Some policemen at this time wore a high leather collar with metal spikes, in case someone tried to choke them.

Today, policemen carry a metal truncheon which can open at the click of a button and extend to about 60 cm. A whistle replaced the rattle, but now, every policeman has a mobile phone, and a flash-lamp instead of the oil lamp. Usually, policemen in Britain don't carry firearms – even today.

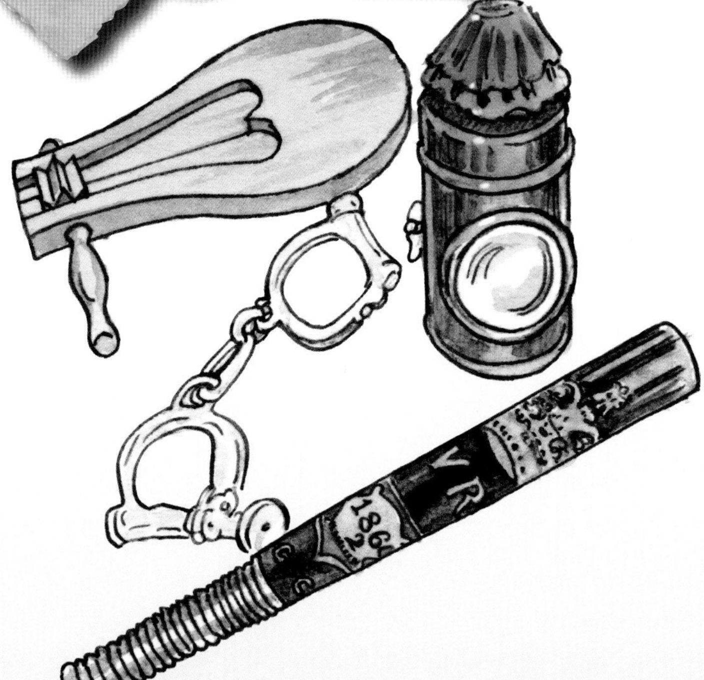

# Capital punishment

The most severe sentence which can be meted out to any criminal is to lose his or her life – that is capital punishment. There were several terrible ways of killing such criminals. Wealthy criminals would be executed, by cutting off their heads with an axe or sword, but hanging with a rope was good enough for the ordinary murderers or thieves. Some were burnt at the stake (tied to a pole), and if a murderer had used poison, he could be boiled alive in oil.

Betraying the king or queen or inciting (starting) a riot were very serious crimes. Such criminals were called traitors. They would be disembowelled (their intestines taken out) and quartered (the body divided into four quarters). Sometimes, there was a further punishment after the person had died. The head would be paraded around on a pole, or the body might be put in a gibbet (a metal frame) to rot. This would be a warning to everyone else not to break the law.

Until about 1800, thieves who stole something to the value of over twelve pence would be hanged.

People loved watching an execution or a hanging. There were two public gallows in Carmarthen – in Pensarn and Johnstown. Three thousand people gathered to watch William Griffith, Newborough, being hanged in Beaumaris in 1830. He was hanged for trying to choke and burn his wife, Mary.

In 1958, Vivian F. Teed was the last person to be hanged in Wales – for murdering the postmaster of Fforest Fach, Swansea. A petition with 1,000 names on it was collected calling for Teed's pardon, because he was mentally ill, but the petition failed to save him.

In 1969, capital punishment was abolished (made away with) in Britain.

It seems that the first person to be hanged, drawn and quartered was Prince Dafydd ap Gruffudd, the brother of Llywelyn the Last. He was sentenced to death because he rose in revolt against Edward I. The four quarters of his body were divided between the cities of Winchester, Northampton, York and Chester.

In 1671, Henry Jones of Monmouthshire was punished extremely cruelly for killing his mother, Grace. He was pressed to death, and he took two days to die.

Only six people were hanged in Beaumaris prison during the eighteenth century. Siân, the daughter of Evan of Llanddaniel, was hanged for stealing, and John Jones was punished by hanging for stealing three sheep in Llanallgo.

It became a custom, after hanging a criminal, to dissect (cut up) his body. David Evans's body was dissected and exhibited to the public in Carmarthen prison in 1829.

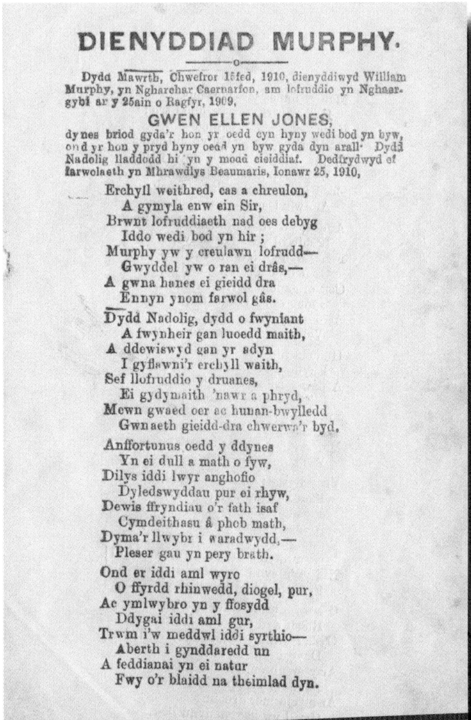

DIENYDDIAD MURPHY.

Dydd Mawrth, Chwefror 15fed, 1910, dienyddiwyd William Murphy, yn Ngharchar Caernarfon, am lofruddio yn Nghaergybi ar y 25ain o Ragfyr, 1909,

GWEN ELLEN JONES,

dynes briod gyda'r hon yr oedd cyn hyny wedi bod yn byw, ond yr hon y pryd hyny oedd yn byw gyda dyn arall. Dydd Nadolig lladdodd hi yn y modd cieiddiaf. Dedfrydwyd ef farwolaeth yn Mhrawdlys Beaumaris, Ionawr 25, 1910,

Erchyll weithred, cas a chreulon,
A gymyla enw ein Sir,
Brwnt lofruddiaeth nad oes debyg
Iddo wedi bod yn hir;
Murphy yw y creulawn lofrudd—
Gwyddel yw o ran ei drâs,—
A gwna hanes ei gieidd dra
Ennyn ynom farwol gâs.

Dydd Nadolig, dydd o fwyniant
A fwynheir gan luoedd maith,
A ddewiswyd gan yr adyn
I gyflawni'r erchyll waith,
Sef llofruddio y druanes,
Ei gydymaith 'nawr a phryd,
Mewn gwaed oer ac hunan-bwylledd
Gwnaeth gieidd-dra chwerwa'r byd.

Anffortunus oedd y ddynes
Yn ei dull a math o fyw,
Dilys iddi lwyr anghofio
Dyledswyddau pur ei rhyw,
Dewis ffryndiau o'r fath isaf
Cymdeithasu â phob math,
Dyma'r llwybr i waradwydd,—
Pleser gau yn pery brath.

Ond er iddi aml wyro
O ffyrdd rhinwedd, diogel, pur,
Ac ymlwybro yn y ffosydd
Ddygai iddi aml gur,
Trwm i'w meddwl iddi syrthio—
Aberth i gynddaredd un
A feddianai yn ei natur
Fwy o'r blaidd na theimlad dyn.

A ballad about the hanging of Murphy for the murder of Gwen Ellen Jones, in Caernarfon in 1910

*Executing a criminal*

Balladeers loved singing ballads about such awful events, and they used to sell their ballads to the crowds gathered to watch a hanging. Thomas Davies of Dowlais composed a popular ballad relating the story of the murder of Tamar Edwards in Merthyr Tudful in 1842. Her son, Richard, was accused of her murder:

A host of Merthyr people
Called out with one cry,
'Don't let us spare the murderer,
But rather, let him die!'

*(translation)*

# Witches

The Tudor and Stuart Ages were very cruel times for witches. About 100,000 witches were burnt at the stake or hanged in Europe, 4,500 in Scotland and about 300 in England. But, in Wales only five witches were hanged.

The first witch to be hanged was Gwen, daughter of Ellis of Denbighshire. They said that she made local people ill through her evil spells. Those who visited her home claimed that she also had a huge fly, and that this fly was the devil. Although Gwen denied this, she was hanged in 1595. The last witch to be hanged was Marged, daughter of Richard of Beaumaris. She was hanged in 1655 for bewitching (casting an evil spell on someone) a local woman.

The ordinary people had their own ways of discovering whether a woman was a witch or not. They also had their own ways of punishing them, without going to a court of law. They would 'swim the witch', by tying the thumb on her right hand to the big toe on her left foot, and the thumb on her left hand to the big toe on her right foot. Then, they would throw her into the river. If she was a witch, she would swim and then, she would be hanged. If she was innocent she would sink and drown, poor thing.

Another cruel punishment would be to tie the woman in a ducking stool and duck her up and down in a lake or river, until she confessed that she was guilty. Once again, several witches would die because of this cruel treatment. In Dolgellau the witches' ducking stool was called '*y gadair goch*' (the red chair).

# Martyrs

During the same period, in the sixteenth and seventeenth centuries, it was a very difficult time for people who disagreed with the religion of the king or queen. One minute, it was dangerous to belong to the Catholic Church and the next minute, it was dangerous to belong to the Church of England. It was also dangerous if you didn't agree with either of these churches! If someone suffered or died for something he or she believed in, then that person was called a martyr.

Queen Mary Tudor, or Bloody Mary, was famous for burning about 275 Protestants in England. But, in Wales only three Protestants were burnt. One of them was the Bishop of St David's, Robert Ferrar, who was burnt at the stake in Carmarthen on March 31, 1555. He faced the death penalty bravely. He raised his arm like a candle in the scorching flames of the fire.

When Elizabeth I became queen, Catholics were persecuted for refusing to attend the Church of England and breaking the laws of Parliament. Richard White from Llanidloes was sentenced to death for being this kind of traitor in 1584. In Wrexham, he was hanged until half dead, then his body was taken down and pieces of it were cut off. Next, the hangman tried to remove his intestines with an axe. White was half-alive throughout this. Then, they cut off his head.

Four other Catholic priests died in a similar way in South Wales in 1679. In 1970, these were made into martyrs and saints by the Pope in Rome.

**John Penry**
The first martyr to be hanged for criticising the Church of England severely was the Welshman, John Penry of Llangamarch, Powys. The bishops didn't like to be criticised in this way. Therefore, Penry was hanged in London on May 29, 1593.

# Hanged by mistake

Some people in Welsh history have been hanged by mistake, and these sad cases have become very well known.

## Dic Penderyn

In June 1831, 10,000 workers from Merthyr Tudful and Dowlais rose in revolt against their iron masters. Unfortunately, during the protest in front of the Castle Hotel, soldiers from Scotland fired at the crowd, killing 24 of them. But, some of the soldiers were also injured – among them Donald Black. Somehow, the name of Richard Lewis, or Dic Penderyn, a 30 year old ironworker was linked to this crime. He was caught and sentenced to death, although he insisted that he was innocent, and although several people supported his story. On August 13, 1831 Dic was hanged in Cardiff prison. As he walked towards the gallows, he shouted (in Welsh), 'Oh Lord, this is an injustice!'

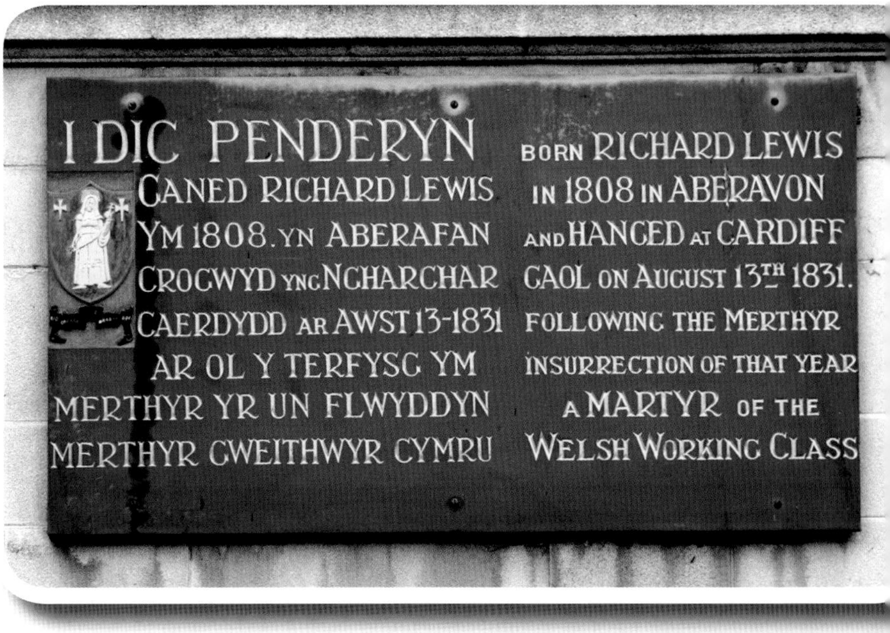


Years later, a man named Ieuan Parker confessed in Pennsylvania, America, that he was guilty of stabbing Black, and that he had fled from Wales because of this. Dic Penderyn was the first martyr of the ironworkers of Merthyr Tudful.

In his novel *The Fire People* (1972), Alexander Cordell describes the hanging of Dic Penderyn dramatically:

'Legend would have it that lightning split the air and that thunder roared as Dic Penderyn died; it is known only that it was raining, and that, in the moment before the trap was pulled, he cried with his face to the sky: 'O Arglwydd, dyma gamwedd!' … And the thunder rolled over the town and the people bowed their heads, they were afraid.'

## Mahmood Matten, the Somalian

Mahmood Matten was a sailor from Somalia, living in Tiger Bay, Cardiff. He was accused of cutting the throat of Lily Volpert, a shopkeeper, in 1952. Although four people claimed that he wasn't near Volpert's shop at the time, within six months, Matten had been found guilty and hanged in Cardiff prison.

For years afterwards Mahmood's mother, Laura Matten, protested and campaigned to prove her son's innocence. At last, in 1998, the family won its appeal and the court agreed that Matten had not had a fair trial.

## Timothy Evans, 10 Rillington Place

Timothy Evans was a Welshman from Merthyr Tudful. He lived with his wife and baby at 10 Rillington Place, North Kensington, London. But, in 1949 he began to say that he had killed his wife and left his baby in someone's care in Wales. When the police searched the house, they found the bodies of Beryl Evans and her dead baby – they had been strangled. Within three months Timothy Evans had been hanged for their murder.

Then, a new tenant came to live in the house. He found six bodies there, including the body of the wife of Christie, Evans' neighbour and landlord. It was obvious that Christie had killed them all, but that he had cast the blame on poor Timothy Evans. In 1953, Christie was hanged, and in 1966, the government pardoned Timothy Evans because he had been hanged by mistake. Timothy Evans's sad story helped to abolish capital punishment in Britain in 1969.

# Shot at dawn

At 7.30 a.m. on Friday, January 5, 1917, Edwin Dyett from Albany Road, Cardiff, was shot dead in France. He was shot by soldiers from his own battalion. Edwin was twenty one years old and had been found guilty of cowardice (not acting bravely) and of deserting (running away from) the battlefield. Therefore, the Army was determined to shoot him, as a warning to others. Three hundred British soldiers were shot in this way during the First World War. Most of them were ordinary soldiers. Only three officers were shot, and Edwin Dyett was one of them. That's why his story is so interesting.

Dyett joined the navy in 1915. During the war he was sent to fight with the army in France. On November 3, 1916, he was fighting in the dreadful battle of the Somme and he was ordered to move forward to the front line. But, for some reason he couldn't find his own unit and he turned back to look for it. On the way, an officer commanded him to return to the front line with a troupe of soldiers. Dyett refused to obey because this officer was less important than him in the army. Then, he lost his way in the fog and did not return to the battlefield for two days. He was accused of being a coward and found guilty. Unfortunately for Dyett, Field Marshall Haig had just decided that, as well as ordinary soldiers, more officers should be punished for deserting the battlefield. Dyett was not allowed to see a doctor nor to appeal against the harsh sentence. The evening before he was shot, he wrote a heart-rending letter to his mother to apologise for 'bringing dishonour (shame) upon you all'.

*A picture from the film 'The Battle of the Somme'*

**A white poppy**
It was a custom to place a white poppy on the breast of a soldier who was to be shot, as a mark of cowardice, and in order to help the shooting squad to aim correctly at his heart.

Altogether, thirteen Welshmen were shot. One of them was William Jones from Glyn Neath of the 9th Battalion of the Royal Welsh Fusiliers. Jones had fled from the battlefield in June 1917. He took a train through France, to England and homewards. In September he went to the police station in Bristol to confess that he had deserted. He was sent back to Belgium at once to stand trial, and was shot at dawn.

**Shot at Dawn**
A movement called 'Shot at Dawn' was established to campaign for pardons for these wretched soldiers. It emphasises that many of them were very young and that they suffered from fear, stress or battle fatigue (tiredness). They were not given a fair trial. In 2001, the movement raised a memorial to them in Staffordshire. In the memorial, 306 wooden posts stand in a semi-circle, with a different soldier's name on each one. In the middle stands the white statue of Herbert Burden, a seventeen year old youth, who could not cope with the battle of Yprés. He was shot at dawn.

In November 2006, the House of Commons agreed to pardon all these soldiers.

# Teaching a hard lesson

From the Middle Ages until the Victorian Age, all kinds of cruel physical punishments were used in Wales to teach criminals a lesson. Prisoners of war would have their limbs chopped off, or their eyes gouged out so that they would never be able to fight again. Many were tortured – by being tied to a gate with their arms and legs outstretched until they were in dreadful pain and willing to confess to anything. Torture was also used to prove witches and to get priests to confess they were Catholics in Elizabeth I's time.

Branding (or burning) parts of the body was another method of punishment. Some would be whipped cruelly. Caernarfon Quarter Sessions Court decided to teach Grace Rowlands a lesson for stealing a sheep in Llanrug in 1686. She was carried to the West Gate in the town. Her clothes were stripped from her waist up. She was tied to a horse and cart, and dragged along the High Street. All the way from West Gate to East Gate, she was whipped until her body was covered in blood.

**Chopping thumbs!**
In 1081, the soldiers in Gruffudd ap Cynan's army were punished by Earl Hugh of Chester by chopping off the thumb on every soldier's right hand. They would never be able to hold a sword or shoot with a bow and arrow again.

**Burning hands!**
A miller from Frogwy, Anglesey, was punished for killing his maidservant in 1735 by burning his hand.

**Gouging eyes!**
In order to avenge (pay back) the Welsh princes, Lord Rhys and Owain Gwynedd, King Henry II gouged out the eyes of 22 hostages (prisoners kept by their enemies in order to help keep the peace). He did this because the princes had raised an army against him in 1165. Two of Owain and two of Rhys's sons were among these poor hostages. Maredudd the Blind, the son of Lord Rhys, had to spend the rest of his life as a monk, rather than a soldier.

There would also be a pillory (stocks for the neck or the feet) in every town. Local people had a great deal of fun mocking criminals in the pillory or stocks, and throwing all kinds of filth and rubbish at them. In the Caernarfon area in 1563, John ab Ieuan was whipped and put in the pillory for stealing an axe. If anyone was left in the pillory for too long, his or her neck could be broken.

**Tomos Glyn Cothi**
When the minister, Tomos Glyn Cothi, was going to be placed in the pillory for supporting the French Revolution around 1813, he bought himself a new coat and waistcoat in order to challenge the authorities, and he sang the Hymn of Freedom loudly. His daughter stood by him the whole time. When a woman threw an egg at Tomos, the crowd attacked her.

In 1975, the United Nations (a society for the countries of the world), announced that it was against mental and physical torture. But, many people still suffer this kind of ill-treatment in the world today.

# Punished ... for being poor

There have been poor people in Wales all through the ages. But, in the Tudor Age, quite suddenly, there were far more poor people wandering the countryside and begging for food than ever before. The government passed several laws to punish them. One punishment was to strip off their clothes, tie them up with a rope and whip them through the village. If a tramp broke the law, a nail would be hammered through his ear to a post in the middle of the town. Vagrants (tramps) would be branded by burning a 'V' shape on their skin with a red-hot iron, so that everyone would know that they were poor.

In 1601, a law was passed which divided vagrants into three categories:

(i) young and healthy – they should work;
(ii) old and sick – they should live in special homes, called almshouses;
(iii) bad and lazy – they should be punished.

Every parish had to raise money to pay for looking after their old and infirm poor. Therefore, it became a custom to force the poor to wear a badge, noting to which parish they belonged. If a vagrant wandered into another parish to beg, he would be sent back to his own parish.

Cardigan Workhouse: the stone-breaking cells

When Margaret, daughter of Ieuan of Ffestiniog, was caught stealing goods worth seven pence in 1557, she was whipped and nailed by her ear to a post in the middle of the town.

### The Workhouse

By 1834, the parishes couldn't cope with the thousands of poor in the land. The government passed the Poor Law to force every tramp – young, old, sick or lazy, who couldn't look after himself or herself, to go to live in a workhouse or poorhouse. The workhouse was like a prison. Families were separated, the food was miserable and everyone had to work hard. If a poor person broke the workhouse rules, he or she would be punished severely.

### The rules of the Workhouse

Here is a verse from a Welsh ballad by R. Williams, Glamorgan, about the workhouse rules:

A husband could not see his wife once the doors were closed,
And mothers couldn't cwtch their young, however much they cared;
Not brother, sister, husband, wife – they cannot share good cheer,
When shut within the workhouse walls, they abandon all things dear.
(*translation*)

Rolant and Betsy Jones of Hen Hafod were allowed to live together in Y Bala workhouse, because they had been married for a very long time. To celebrate this, a picture was taken of the couple for a postcard in 1870.

During the Victorian Age, Mary Davies of Forden workhouse, Powys, was punished for being too noisy. She was placed in a scold's bridle – a metal frame which was placed over her head with a metal tongue to go into her mouth to prevent her from talking at all.

At the beginning of the twentieth century, old people were given an old age pension by the government and there were insurance schemes to help the sick and unemployed. Then, in 1945, the Welfare State was introduced, to support the poor and the needy. No-one is punished for being poor today.

# Down, deep ... in the dungeon

Throwing offenders into prison has been a commo punishment throughout the centuries. There was a prison in every castle. Indeed, there were horrible dungeons in several castles – wet, black holes, with no windows and full of rats. There was a deep dungeon in Denbigh castle, and the Dungeon Tower can still b seen in Pembroke castle today.

Some dangerous prisoners of war were imprisoned fo years. Owain Goch was incarcerated (imprisoned) in Dolbadarn castle for twenty years (from around 1257 until 1277) by his younger brother, Llywelyn the Last. Their nephew, Owain ap Dafydd, spent almost the whole of his life in Bristol castle. After Owain tried to escape, he was kept locked up in a cage every night, li a wild animal.

Britain's most famous prison was the Tower of Londo Many Welsh people, including Gruffudd ap Llywelyn and Catrin Glyndŵr and her children, were imprison there. In 1531, Rhys ap Gruffudd, Lord of Carew, Pembrokeshire, was executed on Tower Hill nearby fo betraying Henry VIII.

When there was no convenient castle, any dark and miserable building would do as a prison. Then, in 177 John Howard travelled around the Welsh prisons. He wanted to reform them. He visited Carmarthen priso and noticed that there were no toilets or running wate no glass in the windows and no firewood or furniture there. He saw men, women and children, all in the same room. He noticed that prisoners had to pay to be released. At last, Howard managed to persuade Parliament to pass an act which would improve Britai prisons. By 1789, there was a new prison in Carmarth and in many other places. This was the beginning of a new era in the history of Britain's prisons.

### Gwenllian

Gwenllian, Llywelyn the Last's only daughter, was not imprisoned in a prison. Instead, she was kept for over fifty years in a nunnery (a home for religious women) in Sempringham, Lincolnshire. The King of England was prepared to pay £20 a year to keep her there so that she would never have children who could fight for Wales.

Dolbadarn castle, where Owain Goch was imprisoned

### Charles Lloyd

Charles Lloyd, a Quaker from Dolobran, Powys, was imprisoned for ten years between 1662 and 1672 for refusing to attend Church of England services. Welshpool jail was incredibly dirty. In the room above, there were thieves and murderers and their stinking sewage seeped down upon Charles Lloyd and his wife, who had joined him in prison.

### *Y Tŷ Crwn* (Round House)

The *Tŷ Crwn* was the jail in Barmouth town, Gwynedd. Here, prisoners would stay until they went to courts. Several drunkards sobered up overnight in the *Tŷ Crwn*.

The Tower of London

### Catrin Glyndŵr

Catrin Glyndŵr was the daughter of Owain Glyndŵr. When Harlech castle fell to the English army in 1408, Catrin and her children were imprisoned in the Tower of London. By 1413, they were all dead and buried in St Swithin's Church nearby. This church was destroyed by a bomb during the Second World War. In 2001, a statue was raised on the site to commemorate (to serve as a memorial to) Catrin and all the other mothers who have suffered because of war.

# Victorian prisons

By the nineteenth century, prisons were better organised, although being put behind bars was still a horrible experience. Many offenders had to do 'hard labour' such as picking oakum (cleaning ropes full of black tar) or working on the treadmill (a drum with a number of steps on it). Prisoners had to climb the treadmill, which turned on the spot, for hours without end. In a day, a prisoner would have climbed about 2,500 metres, twice the height of Snowdon! The energy they produced on the treadmill pumped water into the prison. The women washed clothes, cleaned and picked oakum mainly, though one or two had to work the treadmill too.

If a prisoner offended in prison, he or she would be punished further. Talking, shouting, swearing, whistling and even making signs were punished in Rhuthun prison in 1850. In Beaumaris in 1847, seventeen year old Catherine Morris was locked in a solitary cell without any light and forced to live on bread and water for a whole day, because she was cheeky to the Matron.

Prison food was monotonous. The prisoners had oatmeal porridge for breakfast and supper, bread or potatoes for dinner, and the occasional meal of broth or beef soup.

### The treadmill

In Haverfordwest prison in 1830, the treadmill provided work for 64 prisoners. The doctor there said that mothers who were feeding their babies shouldn't be forced to work on the treadmill.

In 1835, Owen Owens, a prisoner at Caernarfon, asked for a pair of shoes because going on the treadmill barefoot was so painful.

*Picking oakum*

### A nuisance!

Mary Ann Newbury was a nuisance to the keeper of Carmarthen jail in 1845. She refused to pick oakum and she threw her chamber pot at the head of the prison. She was punished by being banished to a solitary cell in chains.

### Rhuthun and Beaumaris prisons

The prisons at Rhuthun and Beaumaris are museums today. Beaumaris prison houses the only treadmill still in working order in Britain. Here too, in 1840, Gaynor Jones was imprisoned for a month with hard labour for stealing two pints of milk.

Jane Roberts was thrown into Rhuthun jail in 1862 for stealing an apron. She had been imprisoned in Flint for stealing a petticoat, and later she was sent to Brixton prison for stealing a nightdress. The prison register notes that Jane had brown hair and green eyes and that she had a small scar on the back of her right hand.

### Washing!

After the Prisons Act of 1865 had been passed, Beaumaris prisoners had to wash themselves once a day and wash their feet once a week.

### Park Prison, Bridgend

Today, there are four prisons and one centre for young offenders in Wales. In Park Prison, Bridgend, there is a toilet and television in every cell, and pool and table tennis tables for the prisoners.

But, the doors are locked and there is no escape.

*Park Prison, Bridgend*
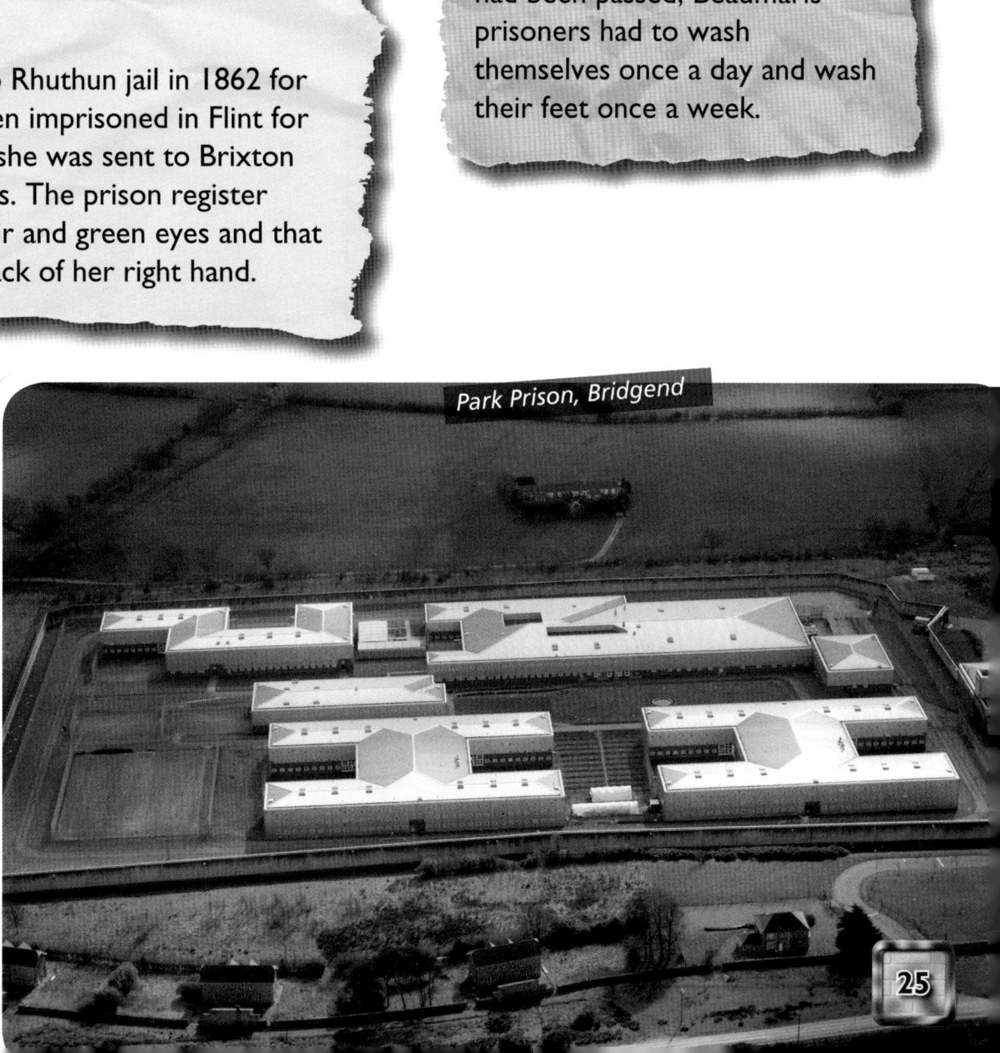

# The great escape!

Stories about prisoners trying to escape from prison, and sometimes succeeding, are full of excitement and adventure.

One of the most famous stories is that of Island Farm Prison, near Bridgend. By the end of the Second World War, around 1,600 Germans, including Nazis from Hitler's army, were imprisoned there. Their guards were soldiers who weren't healthy enough to fight in the British army.

In January 1945, the prisoners began digging a tunnel under the floor of cabin 8. They sawed through the legs of their beds to get timber to hold the roof up, and they used milk tins to make a pipe to carry fresh air into the tunnel. They hid all the spare soil behind a false wall. By March 10, the tunnel was eighteen metres long.

Island Farm today

The Germans had made maps of the area on handkerchiefs, and had found curry powder to deceive the dogs around the camp.
By 2.15 a.m., 65 prisoners had escaped safely under the outer wire of the camp. But, a guard saw the next one trying to escape, and within minutes ten of the free prisoners had been recaptured.

Fifty six prisoners succeeded in escaping. They scattered in all directions. One group managed to steal a car. They travelled to Cardiff to catch a train for Birmingham, but they were caught in the airport there. Another three caught a workers' bus in Cwm-gwrach, some miles away. But, the workers realised who they were because they didn't chat naturally like everyone else. Within seven days, all the prisoners had been recaptured and were back in Island Farm camp.

**Escaping from the Tower of London**

The Tower of London was the King of England's main prison in the Middle Ages. In 1240, during Henry III's reign, Gruffudd, the son of Llywelyn the Great, was a prisoner there. He had quite a luxurious life and the company of his wife Senena, and their son Owain. But, Gruffudd wanted to escape to claim back his kingdom from his half-brother, Dafydd. In the early morning, on March 1, he tied his bedclothes into a long rope and tried to escape through the Tower's high window. Unfortunately, the rope snapped and Prince Gruffudd fell to his death on the ground.

**Coch Bach y Bala**

John Jones, or Coch Bach y Bala as he was called, was considered the champion escaper. He was a famous thief for about 40 years. He succeeded in escaping from his police station cell in Y Bala by walking out of the door when the staff were eating their supper. And in Rhuthun jail, in 1913, he cut a hole in his cell wall and used the bedclothes to climb over the prison wall. But, this time he was shot dead on Nantclwyd Estate, nearby. There was a great deal of interest in his story and postcards showing pictures of his funeral and of the place where he had been shot were sold to local people.

COCH BACH'S FUNERAL AT LLANELIDAN.

# Famous prisons

### The *Clio*

The *Clio* was a British naval ship. In 1877 it was anchored in the Menai Straits, between Bangor and Anglesey. While there it became a remand centre for 250 'gutter children and wastrel boys' – children between eleven and sixteen years old from cities in England mainly. Their parents were either in prison or dead and several of the boys were also thieves.

The boys had to work from six o'clock in the morning until eight at night, learning how to read, write and do arithmetic as well as how to sail. They had to keep the ship shipshape and make their own clothes and boots. It was a pretty harsh life, and 29 of the *Clio's* boys are buried in Llandegfan graveyard. Some died of disease; some fell from the rigging (the ropes holding the sails). Local people called the *Clio* the 'naughty children's ship', and they would warn their own children that if they didn't behave they would be sent there.

*Apprentices on board the* Clio

The 1881 census shows that most of the boys on the *Clio* came from Manchester and London. But, there were some Welsh boys, such as Hugh Edwards of Caernarfon (fifteen years old) and John Roberts of Beaumaris (fourteen years old) among them as well.

**Fron-goch Prison, near Y Bala**
In June 1916, in the middle of the First World War, about 1,863 Irish prisoners were imprisoned in Fron-goch camp, near Y Bala. They had risen in revolt against the British government and were fighting for a Free Ireland.

The Fron-goch prisoners were determined men. As prisoners of war, they insisted upon their right to wear their own clothes. They were also committed to the cause of a Free Ireland and while at the camp they plotted how they could rekindle the rebellion. One of the prisoners was Michael Collins who became the head of the Free Ireland army. He was surprised to hear the local people in Y Bala speaking Welsh naturally, and he decided to learn his own language, Irish. By Christmas 1916, most of the Irishmen had been released.

*Michael Collins*

**Henllan camp, South Ceredigion**
During the Second World War, many Italian and German prisoners were imprisoned around Wales. Cabins near the village of Henllan, Ceredigion, were used as a jail for Italian prisoners. During the day they would wear brown uniforms with yellow circles on them, and work on the local farms.

*Henllan camp today*

*The chapel in Henllan camp*

One of the prisoners was the artist, Mario Ferlito. He decided to paint a picture of Jesus Christ's Last Supper on the wall of the little chapel at the camp. He used fruit and vegetable juices to get the right dyes. Other prisoners created candlestick holders from beef and cocoa tins. You can visit the chapel today and marvel at the work of the Italian prisoners of war.

# Imprisoned ... far overseas

Between the seventeenth century and the Victorian Age a number of Welsh people were exiled, or transported (punished by sending them to 'prisons' overseas). The British government wanted to get rid of dangerous criminals, by sending them as far away as possible from home. In America, the prisoners worked without pay. They would have to work on tobacco plantations in Virginia and Georgia for several years before being released.

But, after America had freed itself from Britain at the end of the eighteenth century, the British government decided to open up the vast continent of Australia as a prison – with no walls except the great ocean. The first fleet of offenders arrived in Sydney harbour in 1788. If these prisoners were lucky, they would work for a kind master. But, if they were unlucky, their master could be hard and cruel. At the end of their term as prisoners, some would come home to Wales, but many stayed in the new country and became hardworking and successful members of society there.

In 1773, Margaret Thomas of Llanbedr-goch, Anglesey, was transported to America for seven years, for stealing a cloak and an apron.

Benjamin Clark of Glamorgan, a 24 year old man, was exiled to Australia for seven years in 1852-3 for stealing a piece of brass worth ten shillings (50 pence).

**John Frost**

This is how John Frost described the whip used to punish disobedient criminals:

> 'The cord was put into salt water... it was then put in the sun to dry. By this process, it became like wire, the eighty-one knots cutting the flesh as if a saw had been used.'

Frost was exiled to Van Diemen's Land, Australia for helping to organise the Chartist riot (a riot by a movement which campaigned for every man to have the vote and other rights) in Newport in 1839. He worked as a clerk and a teacher there. In 1856, he returned to Britain a free man.

## Zephaniah Williams

Another of the Newport Chartists, Zephaniah Williams, was lucky enough to discover coal in Van Diemen's Land after years as a prisoner there. He became quite wealthy, and his wife and daughter travelled from Wales to join him in 1854, after fourteen years apart.

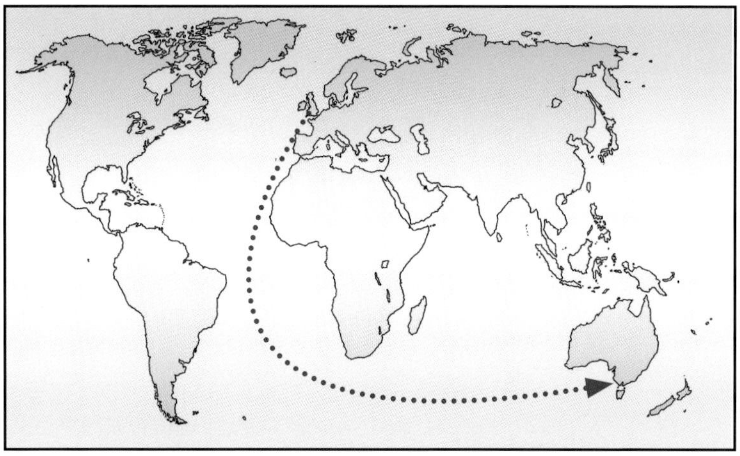

There were far more men than women in Australia and they wanted to start families to farm and develop the new country. Therefore, very often, if a strong young girl had committed a rather insignificant crime in Britain, she would be punished by being transported to prison overseas, although very often she didn't deserve such a harsh punishment. On arrival in Australia, the less fortunate girls would be sent to dreadful prisons or factories, such as Parramatta Factory, near Sydney. Criminals and single men would come there to choose a wife. The girls would stand in rows, and the men would walk up and down eyeing them. Then, one of the men would drop a handkerchief at the feet of his chosen bride. If she picked up the handkerchief, they would be married at once.

# Prisoners of war

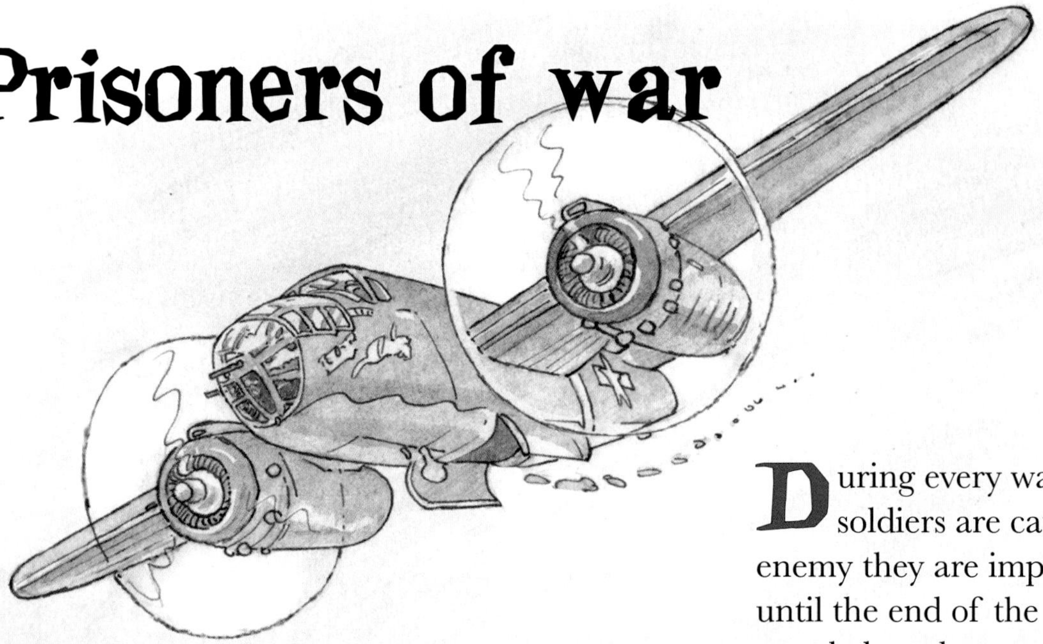

During every war, if ordinary soldiers are caught by the enemy they are imprisoned, often until the end of the war. Many Welsh people have been prisoners all over the world, especially during the two World Wars in the twentieth century. And they have amazing stories to tell.

**John Escott: a prisoner in Burma**

John Escott from Cardiff was a prisoner of war in a Japanese prison during the Second World War. For over 60 years he didn't utter a word about this painful experience. Then, he decided to tell the terrible story. He worked on the famous Burmese railway, which was called The Death Railway, and where the guards and officers were incredibly cruel. One day, an American plane flew over the camp dropping leaflets to say that the camp was to be bombed. The prisoners formed the shape of a 'V' (for victory) on the landing strip to warn the pilot. He realised who they were and flew away without bombing the camp.

## Elias Henry Jones: a prisoner during the First World War

Elias Henry Jones from Aberystwyth was a prisoner in Yozgad prison, in Turkey, during the First World War. In 1920, he published a book called *The Road to En-Dor*, describing his ordeal there. The prison was surrounded by mountains and a desert, and it was impossible to escape over land. In the camp, the prisoners learnt how to cook and they organised games, an orchestra and mathematics, French and other lessons to pass the time. But, Jones wanted to escape. He, and an Australian prisoner called Hill, decided upon a very strange plan. First of all they succeeded in persuading the prisoners and officers that they could talk to spirits, and that a ghost would tell them where some treasure had been buried. The ghost spoke Welsh! Jones recited an old Welsh poem to try to convince them. But, this plan failed. Therefore, Jones and Hill pretended they were going mad. They almost died when they tried to hang themselves. At last, the officers had had enough of this strange pair and they were taken to a hospital in Istanbul, and then sent home in October 1918. Within six weeks the war was over and all the other prisoners were also free!

*British prisoners of war in the Far East during the Second World War*

Imperial War Museum

## Brynly Owen Thomas: a Japanese prisoner of war

Many Welsh soldiers spent time during the Second World War as Japanese prisoners of war. Brynly Owen Thomas from Swansea, for example, was captured in Java in 1942. The Japanese guards were atrociously cruel. If a prisoner looked at the face of a Japanese soldier he would be beaten with bamboo sticks. People were starved and tortured for doing the most insignificant things. One out of every four prisoner died from cruelty, disease or starvation. The war against Japan came to an end on August 15, 1945, after America had dropped nuclear bombs on Hiroshima and Nagasaki.

Today, despite the extreme cruelty of these prisons, a society has been established to bring British prisoners of war and the Japanese guards who maltreated and imprisoned them face to face once more.

# Choosing to be behind bars

It's strange to think that some people break the law on purpose and choose to be punished by going to prison. Many people in Welsh history have done so because they believe that the law is unfair. They choose to commit a serious crime in order to draw dramatic attention to a special cause.

**Winning the vote**

It was the campaign for votes for women which drove Margaret Haig Thomas (Lady Rhondda) to join the Suffragette movement (a movement which believed that the law had to be broken in order to win the vote) at the beginning of the twentieth century. In order to draw attention to the cause, she threw a bomb into a post box in Newport in 1913. Margaret chose to go to prison, though her husband would have been able to pay to set her free. In prison, she went on a hunger strike, but after five days without food she was set free.

**Refusing to fight or help the war effort**

During the First World War it was a serious offence for a soldier, who had been called up to fight, to refuse to do so. But, some believed that fighting and killing was wrong. These would be brought before a military tribunal (court) and imprisoned. Gwenallt, the poet from Cwm Tawe, was imprisoned in Wormwood Scrubs and Dartmoor because he refused to fight for the king. He wrote a novel, *Plasau'r Brenin* (The King's Palaces) describing his lonely experiences there.

Ithel Davies from Mallwyd described the way he was maltreated because he refused to help the war effort. He was imprisoned in Mold jail and tied into a straight jacket for six hours so that he couldn't bend or move. Then, an officer attacked him and broke his nose.

Some were punished during the Second World War too. Iris Cooze from Abercynon was not prepared to help the war effort because she was a Christian, and she was thrown into Cardiff prison for a month. After her release, people shouted 'Conshi' (conscientious objector) at her. But, she was glad she had stood up for her beliefs.

**For the language**

Many Welsh people have campaigned for the rights of the Welsh language during the last fifty years, and have been punished for doing so. Angharad Tomos was imprisoned in Holloway in 1983. In her book, *Yma o Hyd* (Still Here), she describes life in jail:

'We mend the men's clothes… through the day, every day… Miles of poor blue and white striped material… in the end you come to the conclusion that they don't do anything all day except rip their clothes so that we have to mend them.'

(*translation*)

*Angharad Tomos*

In 2005, a young girl called Gwenno Teifi from Llanfihangel-ar-Arth, decided to break into Radio Carmarthenshire (*Radio Sir Gâr*)'s offices and make a mess there. She wanted to draw attention to the fact that there was very little Welsh on this channel. She refused to pay the fine and was sent to prison in Gloucester for five days. The other prisoners couldn't understand why she was there at all.

# Exciting forensic developments

During the last hundred years, scientists have found exciting forensic techniques to help the police solve serious crimes.

**DNA**

DNA is a chemical present in almost every cell in our body. It decides the colour of our hair and our eyes. In the beginning a sample the size of a five pence piece had to be collected to get a result, but, now a little spit or a hair is enough.

Since about 1984 the police have depended a great deal upon DNA samples from offenders' and victims' bodies in order to solve serious crimes.

**The Llandarcy murders**

During 1973 three young girls were murdered, one after the other, in a wood in Llandarcy, near Swansea. Although the police investigated the crimes carefully and gathered very many fingerprints, they did not succeed in catching the murderer. Then, in the year 2000, after further developments in the forensic field, the police were lead by a DNA sample to a man who used to live in Swansea. But, he had been dead for twelve years. They exhumed his body (lifted it from its grave) and discovered that he was the murderer. His name was Joe Kappen from Port Talbot. At last, after 30 years, the girls' families could close the door on this very sad chapter in their history.

## The case of Lynette White

Lynette White was twenty years old when she was murdered in Cardiff in 1988. Unfortunately, three men were imprisoned by mistake for the crime in 1990, but, after two years they were released. But, the murderer was also free, although the police had taken thousands of DNA samples.

Then, ten years later, they decided to search for further DNA samples – under the paint in Lynette's home. They discovered the murderer's DNA there. Very strangely, the police had a record of a very similar DNA – which belonged to a young lad. But, he hadn't even been born in 1988. The police examined the boy's DNA carefully and discovered one of his relatives – Jeffrey Gafoor of Llanharan. When Gafoor heard that the police were on his trail he admitted that he had murdered Lynette White.

## The body in the carpet

This is an excellent example of scientists co-operating to solve a murder. In 1989 builders found a body wrapped in a carpet under the patio in a house in Cardiff. The police had no idea whose body it was. By studying the insects on the carpet scientists could show that the person had been dead for about ten years. Then, a dentist succeeded in proving, by examining the teeth, that it was the body of a girl of about fifteen years old.

The next step was for an artist to make a model of the head. The model was shown on the *Crimewatch* programme on television. At once, two people rang in to suggest that it could be that of Karen Price, who had disappeared in 1981. After comparing the body's DNA and that of Karen's family's DNA, the police confirmed this theory. Within a year two men had been accused of murdering Karen Price.

# Punishment in schools

Every school has its own rules and when these are broken pupils have to be punished. In the Victorian Age children were punished severely for all kinds of things, such as arriving late, talking too much or fighting in the yard. Wearing a fool's cap and standing in the corner was one punishment for presenting poor work. Another punishment was to lock a child in a cellar or in a dark cupboard for hours.

The favourite punishment was for teachers to beat pupils with a cane. Boys were usually punished in this way but girls could also be caned. The pupils believed that caning would be less painful if they pulled out one hair, placed it across the palm of the hand, and spat on it.

In 1901, the government decided that every school had to keep a Punishment Book to record every case of caning pupils. Only the headmaster was allowed to use the cane – and only on the older boys. But, the Punishment Books also show that not every teacher believed in using the cane at all.

By 1987, the government had abolished the use of the cane and every other kind of corporal (physical) punishment. The most severe punishment which can be meted out by a school today is to exclude a pupil from school.

**Trefor School Punishment Book**
Trefor School (Gwynedd)'s Punishment Book for the year 1909 shows that the headmaster, J. E. Williams, had used the cane 267 times. Indeed, 'the old schoolmaster was a devil of a man'.

**Punishing Rhys Lewis**
Robin the Soldier, the schoolteacher in Daniel Owen's famous novel *Rhys Lewis*, had a very wild temper, especially if anyone laughed at his wooden leg. Rhys was punished severely for doing so – 'the next minute the cane was cutting me all ways – across my head, my neck, my back, my legs… A dark night came over me.'

(*translation*)

*A pupil being caned*

**The Welsh Not**

The Welsh Not was a piece of wood with the letters 'W.N.' on it, to be hung with a cord around the neck.

When O. M. Edwards was a pupil at the church school in Llanuwchllyn about 1865, he saw the Welsh Not in use. He describes how a child would be punished for speaking Welsh. Another child would carry tales to the teacher about this child. Then the teacher would put the Welsh Not around his neck until he heard another child speaking Welsh. At the end of the school day the child with the W.N. around his or her neck would be caned on the hand.

When O. M. Edwards became Chief Inspector of Schools in 1907 he insisted that the Welsh language should be taught in the schools of Wales.

In 1847, when examining schools in Wales, an Inspector noticed the 'Welsh Stick' in Llandyrnog School in the Vale of Clwyd. But, as he said, the children didn't have any choice about speaking Welsh because they couldn't speak English anyway!

Many countries have used something similar to the Welsh Not to make one language superior to another. In the 1950s in Kenya, Africa, children who used their own language, Gikuyu, instead of English, the official language, were forced to wear a piece of metal with the words 'I am stupid. I am a donkey' on it.

# Drug smuggling

Smuggling has been going on in Wales throughout the centuries. Three or four centuries ago tobacco, arms, salt and spirits such as rum and brandy were the main goods being smuggled, but, today it's drugs which lure smugglers to break the law. There are several famous stories about drug smuggling and Wales.

**'Operation Sealbay'**

This campaign was called 'Operation Sealbay' because the police found a centre for smugglers in a beautiful bay where seals swam, near Moylgrove, on the northern coast of Pembrokeshire. A local fisherman, Andrew Burgess, warned the police that something strange was afoot on the beach, after he had noticed large black plastic bags there. When the police investigated the area on June 19, 1983, they found thousands of pounds' worth of expensive radio gear, motor boats and tents hidden under the canvasses. Then, they discovered a room dug into the beach with its door concealed by stones. The police watched the beach for months and at last they succeeded in catching the gang of five men who were plotting to smuggle drugs into Britain through North Pembrokeshire.

Police with their dogs looking for drugs

**'Operation Julie'**
Residents of the country villages of Carno, Powys and Blaencaron, Ceredigion, were astounded on March 26, 1977 when they saw policemen searching two houses in the area. In a laboratory in Carno a chemist called Richard Kemp and his partner, Doctor Christine Bott, had been busy producing pure drugs worth £100 million. They stored them at Blaencaron. The police came across the drugs by chance when Kemp was involved in a serious car accident. When searching his vehicle they found a piece of paper explaining how to make drugs. About 800 police took part in this operation and it was called 'Operation Julie' after one of the policewomen in the team.

**'Operation Capsule'**
In February 2006 the last members of a gang of twenty smugglers from South Wales were caught and imprisoned for over 121 years. The gang leader was Darren Owen from Ton-teg, who was caught escaping across the border from France into Spain with a car full of money. The gang had been selling drugs throughout South Wales and living in a very luxurious way before they were caught.

**Howard Marks: a very strange smuggler**
Marks is one of the strangest criminals! He was caught in 1988 and sentenced to 25 years in Terre Haute, Indiana, one of America's most notorious (bad) prisons. Marks comes from Kenfig Hill near Bridgend. Although he had a degree in nuclear physics from Oxford University he decided that he would prefer to make money by smuggling hashish and cannabis from Asia into Europe and America. In order to do so he had 25 different companies, 43 different names and identities, and 89 different telephone numbers. Marks succeeded in deceiving the world's police forces for fourteen years.

Marks spent seven years behind bars, and since being released he's written a book, *Mr Nice*, and has sung on an album by the famous Welsh group, the Super Furry Animals.

# The century of the car

During the twentieth century cars changed everyone's lives, including those of the police force. From about 1935 onwards, the police had cars, and they didn't have to depend upon a bike or a motorbike to catch a criminal quickly. By the 1960s hundreds of cars patrolled the roads. Not many police could now be seen walking the streets of our towns and villages, chatting to people and getting to know their beat.

With all the cars on the roads, new offences, such as driving too fast, driving dangerously and drink driving have evolved. Several laws have been passed to improve travellers' safety. Now, there are laws regarding wearing seatbelts and passing the driving test and laws to restrict speeding. If someone breaks these laws, he or she can be brought before the courts and fined, or even sent to prison.

One of the first car accidents in Wales occurred in Llanishen, Cardiff, in 1903 when a 75 year old woman was killed by a learner driver. The car was travelling at between five and eight miles an hour.

## Speeding

- One of the first to be fined (£1) for speeding was Harold Bater, the chauffeur of Anglesey's Marquis, in 1902. A witness said that the car was travelling so fast (at 25 miles per hour) that he couldn't see the driver. The Justice of the Peace said that the Welsh people could be divided into two categories of people – car drivers and those who were going to be knocked down by a car.

- One group of drivers caught speeding in the Neath area were the World Rally Championship's drivers in 2002. One champion, Freddie Loix from Belgium, received a fine of £1,750 and was banned from driving for six months. But, he could still drive on the public roads during the rally itself.

- Richard Brunstrom, the Chief Constable of North Wales Police, became famous for his campaign to catch speeding drivers. In 2003-04, fines worth £3.4 million were collected through speed cameras on the roads of North Wales. Now, some fast drivers are being sent for extra driving lessons instead of being fined.

- In 2006, a woman from Mold was fined £200 for dangerous driving. The police had caught her driving in the Pwllheli area, and putting on her make-up with both hands at the same time.

**D for '*Dysgwr*'**
Eirug Wyn of Deiniolen was seventeen years old when he broke the law in 1967 by putting the red letter 'D' for '*Dysgwr*' on his car instead of 'L' for Learner. Eventually he won his fight for the right to use the Welsh language.

**Joyriding**
By the end of the twentieth century stealing cars for fun had become a dangerous hobby among young people in Wales. The film *Twin Town*, filmed in Swansea in the mid 1990s, is about joyriding. The two main characters were played by brothers Rhys and Llŷr Evans. But in fact, joyriding is an old hobby. In 1929 two youths from Narberth, Pembrokeshire, stole a car and drove it for fun towards Crymych. But they had an accident *en route* and were caught by the police.

Published by CAA, Aberystwyth University, The Old College, King Street, Aberystwyth, SY23 2AX
(www.caa.aber.ac.uk).

Sponsored by the Welsh Assembly Government.

ISBN 978-1-84521-284-1



**Editor:** Fflur Pughe
**Photographs and Copyright Research:** Helen Emanuel Davies and Fflur Pughe
**Designer:** Richard Huw Pritchard
**Printers**: The IMEX Group (01792 704 880)



## Acknowledgements

Thank you to the following for permission to reproduce materials in this publication:

By permission of the National Library of Wales – p. 3, 5
Carmarthenshire Archives Service – p. 3
Photolibrary Wales – p. 5, 15, 23, 25, 26, 41
The Judge's Lodging, Presteigne, Powys – p. 6, 7
Glamorgan Record Office / South Wales Police Museum – p. 8
Gwynedd Archives Service – p. 11, 21, 28
Mary Evans Picture Library – p. 12, 23
By kind permission of the publisher Blorenge Books – p.15
Imperial War Museum Q 70167 – p. 17; HU 4569 – p. 33
Ceredigion Museum – p. 21
Getty Images: Hulton Archive – p. 25, 38
Topfoto/HIP/British Library – p. 27
Bangor University Record Office – p. 27
Topfoto – p. 29
Cadw. Crown Copyright – p. 29
Mrs. J. E. Harding Rolls, Rockfield House, Rockfield, Monmouthshire
via Gwent Record Office – p. 30, 31
Y Lolfa (extract from *Yma o Hyd* by Angharad Tomos; photograph by Marian Delyth) – p. 35
By permission of Hughes a'i Fab (extract from *Rhys Lewis* by Daniel Owen) – p. 38
National Museum Wales – p. 39

Every effort has been made to trace and acknowledge ownership of copyright. The publishers will be pleased to make suitable arrangements with any copyright holders who have not been contacted.

Thank you to Carys Edwards, Gwyn Gruffydd, Nia Gruffydd, Cathryn Gwynn and Sarah Rees
for their valuable guidance.

Thank you to the following schools for taking part in the trialling process:

Ysgol Uwchradd Caereinion, Llanfair Caereinion
Ysgol Gynradd Nefyn, Nefyn, Pwllheli
Ysgol Gymunedol Talybont, Talybont, Aberystwyth
Ysgol Gyfun Ystalyfera, Ystalyfera, Swansea

Also available is *Trosedd a Chosb*, a Welsh medium version of this publication.